Big Bug

and

On the Map

By Jenny Moore

Illustrated by
Camilla Frescura

The Letter B

Trace the lower and upper case letter with a finger. Sound out the letter.

Down,
up,
around

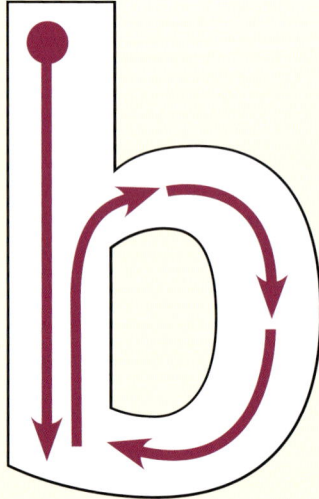

Down,
up,
around,
around

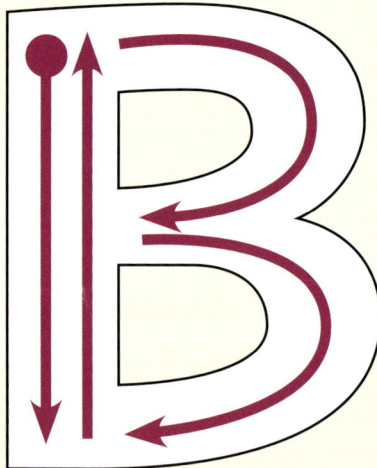

Some words to familiarise:

big

bug

High-frequency words:

a   the   no   I   it   is

Tips for Reading 'Big Bug'

- Practise the words listed above before reading the story.

- If the reader struggles with any of the other words, ask them to look for sounds they know in the word. Encourage them to sound out the words and help them read the words if necessary.

- After reading the story, ask the reader what colour the biggest bug was.

Fun Activity

Discuss what animals are bigger than you are!

Big Bug

No. I am a big bug.

9

No, I am big.
A big, fat bug.

11

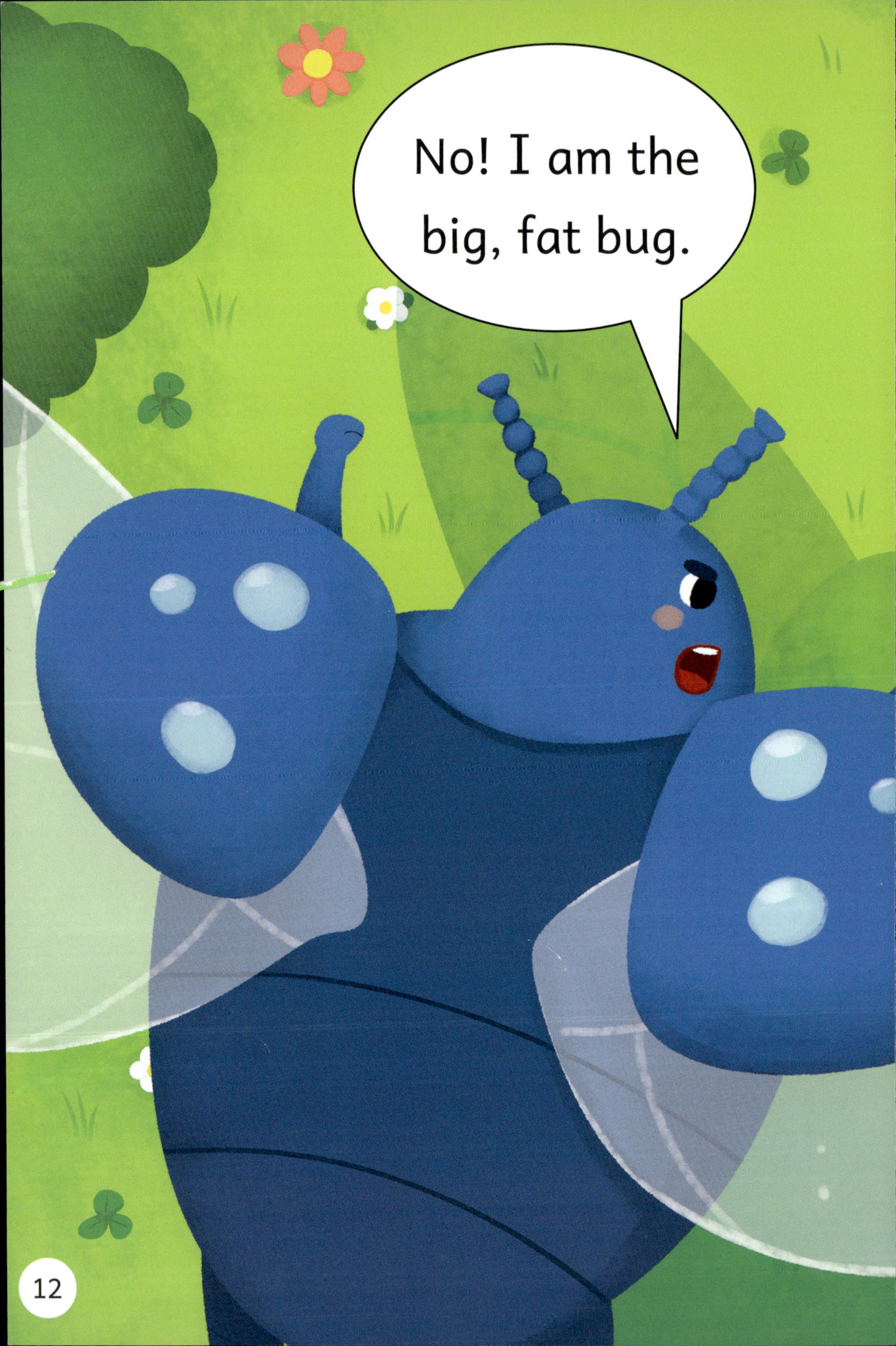
No! I am the
big, fat bug.

A bug!

Is it big?

No. It is not a big bug.

BIG BOOK
of BUGS

The Letter M

Trace the lower and upper case letter with a finger. Sound out the letter.

*Down,
up,
around,
down,
up,
around,
down*

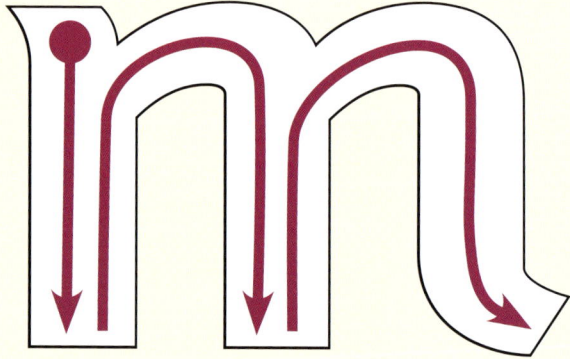

*Down,
up,
down,
up,
down*

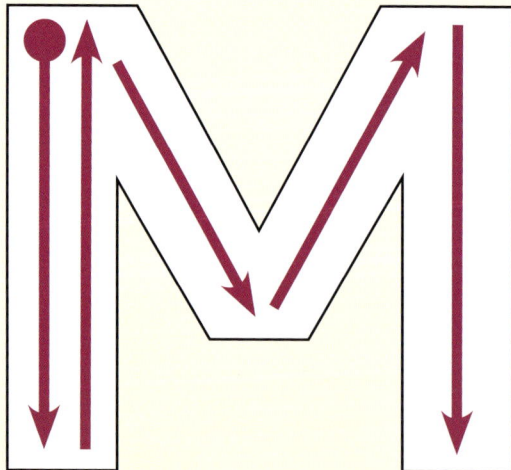

Some words to familiarise:

Sal map nut

High-frequency words:

has   a   is   on   the

Tips for Reading 'On the Map'

- Practise the words listed above before reading the story.

- If the reader struggles with any of the other words, ask them to look for sounds they know in the word. Encourage them to sound out the words and help them read the words if necessary.

- After reading the story, ask the reader how Sal found her nut.

Fun Activity

Make a treasure map!

On the Map

Sal has a map.

A hill is on the map.

A mill is on the map.

A hut is on the map.

A gap is on the map.

28

A nut is on the map.

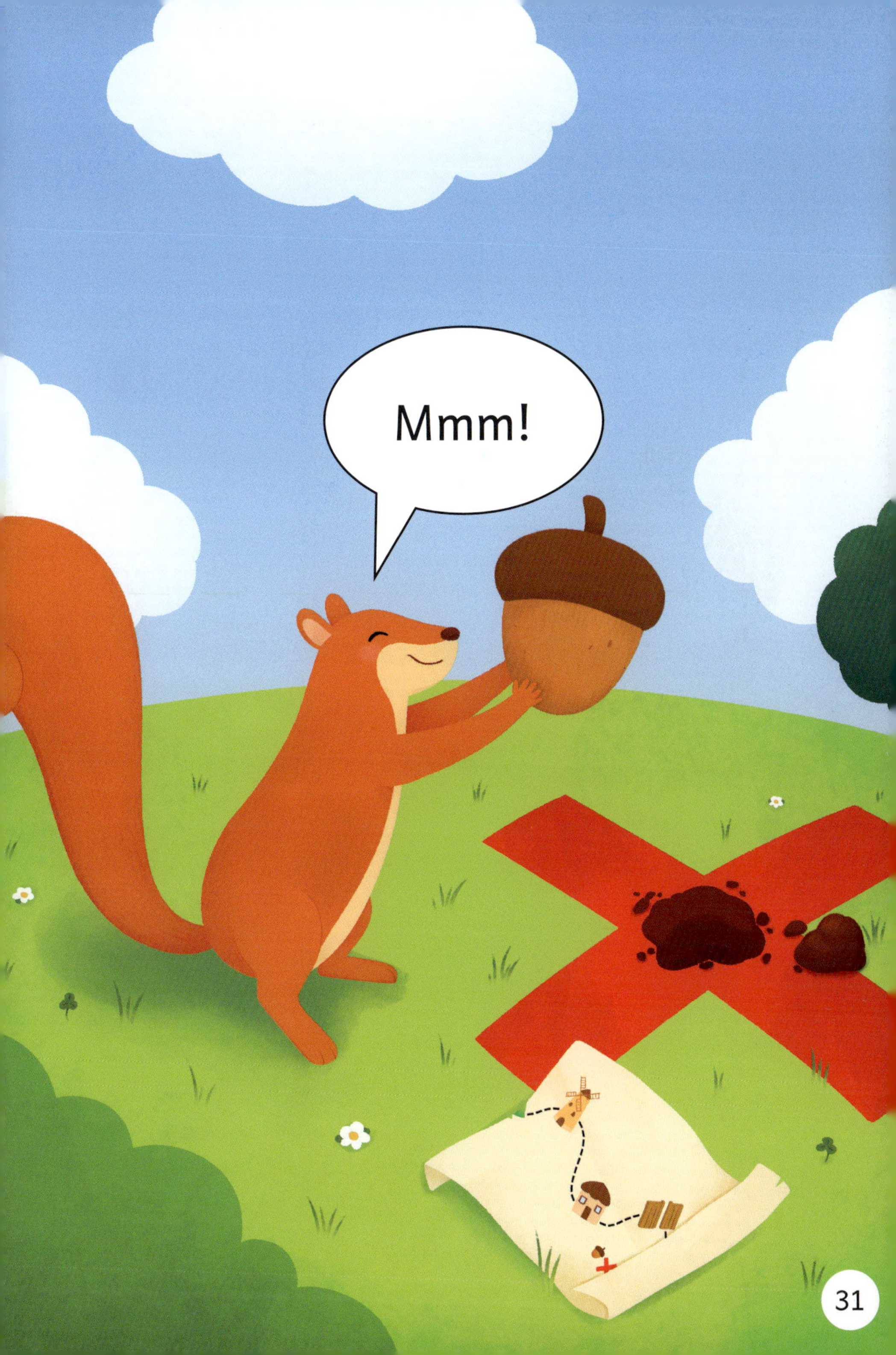
Mmm!

Book Bands for Guided Reading

The Institute of Education book banding system is a scale of colours that reflects the various levels of reading difficulty. The bands are assigned by taking into account the content, the language style, the layout and phonics. Word, phrase and sentence level work is also taken into consideration.

Maverick Early Readers are a bright, attractive range of books covering the pink to white bands. All of these books have been book banded for guided reading to the industry standard and edited by a leading educational consultant.

Pink

Red

Yellow

Blue

Green

Orange

Turquoise

Purple

Gold

White

Cool Duck and Lots of Hats
by Elizabeth Dale
Illustrated by Anni Caplan

Catch It, Jess! and Cat Nap
by Katie Dale
Illustrated by Kasia Dudziuk

The Space Race
by Jenny Jinks
Illustrated by Serena Lombardo

Pirates Don't Drive Diggers
by Alex English Illustrated by Duncan Beedie

A Right Royal Mess

To view the whole Maverick Readers scheme, visit our website at www.maverickearlyreaders.com

Or scan the QR code above to view our scheme instantly!

Big Bug

and

On the Map

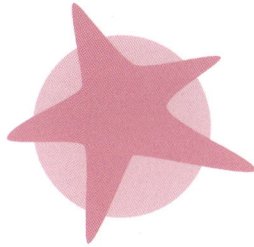

Maverick

Early Readers

'Big Bug' and 'On the Map'
An original concept by Jenny Moore
© Jenny Moore 2022

Illustrated by Camilla Frescura

Published by MAVERICK ARTS PUBLISHING LTD
Studio 11, City Business Centre, 6 Brighton Road,
Horsham, West Sussex, RH13 5BB
© Maverick Arts Publishing Limited May 2022
+44 (0)1403 256941

A CIP catalogue record for this book is available at the British Library.

ISBN 978-1-84886-873-1

Maverick
publishing
www.maverickbooks.co.uk

Pink

This book is rated as: Pink Band (Guided Reading)
It follows the requirements for Phase 2 phonics.
Most words are decodable, and any non-decodable words are familiar,
supported by the context and/or represented in the artwork.